Start with the Heart

TEN PRACTICES FOR RELATIONSHIP BUILDING

Frankie Blackburn

ACKNOWLEDGMENTS

William Traynor

Judith Brooks

Leigh Harwood

Mary Jeanne Brown

Avery Harwood

Luisa Montero

Joni Hirsch Kaden

Marshall Pollard

Charles Tookey

Mtende Roll

Jan Thrope

Sandra Mikush

Paulette Millichap

Christine Clifton

All of the forgoing contributed wisdom, skill and moral support in this enterprise.

First edition. First Printing

Illustrations © 2022 Frankie Blackburn

Editorial Services: Lyn Fairchild Hawks at Success Stories

Cover and text design: Carl Brune

Printed in the USA

ISBN: 979-8-218-11917-1

Subjects: Interpersonal Relations, Civics and Citizenship, Communication and Social Skills, Personal Growth, Self-Help

Frankie Blackburn
PO Box 220, Saxapahaw, NC 27340
301-717-1800

www.startwiththeheartbooks.com   www.trustedspacepartners.com

Gratitude for Community-Building Friends

To develop the practices and collect the stories shared in this book, I interviewed a diverse[1] group of over 50 people who are intentional relationship builders. These folks inhabit a multitude of spaces where they work and live as community organizers, teachers, nurses, librarians, elected officials, nonprofit and government leaders, artists, social workers, realtors and small business owners. I am very grateful for their time and insights. I love thinking about all the relationships flowing from their intentional steps and actions. Thank you! You inspire and motivate us!

Yerodin Avent	Molly Jackman	Reemberto Rodriguez
Kim Bishop	Mark Joseph	Mtende Roll
Stan Botts	Joni Hirsch Kaden	Shawnn Shears
Mary Jeanne Brown	Erica McAdoo	Laura Steinberg
Sebastian Brown	Ray Moreno	Kathy Stevens
Monica Buitrago	Luisa Montero	Jalina Suggs
Robert Byrd	Mary Murphy	Lisa Jean Sylvia
Carmen Centeno	Sara Mussie	Jan Thrope
Tasha Espendez	Tom O'Brien	Julie Todd
Diana Garcia	Jayne Park	Bill Traynor
Gwendolyn Garth	Julia Park	Chuck Tookey
Laura Hagmann	Donna Poe	Shelley Voss
Noelle Haile	Marshall Pollard	Kristin Wallace
Avery Harwood	Phillipe Celestin	Chris Wilhelm
Leigh Harwood	Pat Robinson	

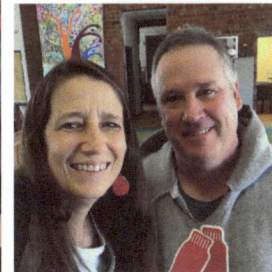

1 Some folks didn't mind being identified by race, ethnicity, sexual orientation, age, and/or gender; others preferred not to. So you will see that sometimes I specify identities and other times I do not. I also honored specific requests for how to identify by race, when offered.

Are you sometimes lonely and wish you had more friends?

Are you searching for a different set of friends, ones who bring out the best in you?

Are you challenged by getting to know people who are different than you?

If you answered yes to any of these questions, this book offers some practical ideas for you.

Why Focus on Relationship Building?

I have spent my life building relationships, especially relationships with people different from me. Every day I connect as a co-worker, mom, friend, and neighbor. I am also what you call a professional community organizer. I feel much happier, more secure, and better about myself when actively cultivating friends, especially friends who bring me a new perspective or a different set of skills or life experiences. And I have listened to hundreds of people from different backgrounds testify that overcoming the fear of intentionally reaching out to others leads them to a better place in life.

I believe with all my heart in Martin Luther King's vision of a "beloved community" ("The King Philosophy – Nonviolence 365 ®"), a world where all people belong and thrive.[2]

I have made and still make mistakes in my quest to build relationships with others. I have gathered many hard lessons learned. I know well the fear of reaching out to someone new or managing a challenging moment as our relationship evolves. And I still avoid some people and draw boundaries when needed.

2   See Appendix A for a link to The Thrive Network and their vision of a beloved community: "love and justice have prevailed; people from all walks of life are valued, respected, and treated with dignity; all people feel safe, cared for, and connected; we share our gifts and resources openly with one another, peacefully resolving conflict, living in balance with nature, and embodying lives of meaning, joy and well-being" (Thrive).

I used to never think about the practice of relationship building. It was just one of those things you did ... naturally. As the years went by, I observed that making connections was becoming more and more difficult for myself, my children, and my co-workers. Many have written about why this seems true.

It's our growing diversity.
It's racism and white supremacy.
It's the internet and social media.
It's our political polarization.
It's consumerism.

I believe that we have no choice but to figure out how to honor, respect, and know "the others" in our midst. Our world is on the edge of destruction precisely because we are afraid to build the bridges necessary to heal, transform, connect.

Sadly, I know many people who suffer greatly, mainly due to living in isolation, fear, and anger. I also see many community improvement efforts fail because the workers involved are too closed off from the neighbors who should be involved and leading it. Most frequently, I see organizations of all types, private and nonprofit, implode because they failed to understand the value of cultivating relationships across their many differences as a group of people.

The first half of my professional career was devoted to building and managing mixed-income housing communities. I'll never forget how scared I was standing in front of a room of residents who lived in a run-down apartment complex. The small nonprofit I worked for had just bought the building to rehab it into a nicer place to live. I knew the room of frustrated lower-income residents, virtually all of whom were recent immigrants from three different cultural groups in Eastern Africa, did not trust our promises to work in partnership with them. And I didn't know how to build relationships with them or to gain their trust.

I lucked into finding the best and most committed language interpreter ever. He guided me step by step in showing up at each door—over and over again for 18 months—and slowly demonstrating to the residents that we, the building owners, were to be trusted.

After completing the rehab, I was devastated when the leaders of my nonprofit rejected my proposal to share the annual budgeting process with the residents. I believe they wanted to do the right thing but were afraid of losing control over key expense items to people who—in their minds—do not have the requisite expertise. Since then, I have been on a mission to help institutional leaders feel less fear in sharing their positional power with those who bring them tremendous personal power, wisdom, and skill.

We must create a new just and joyful way of living, with collective systems to support it. And as a white woman, I believe white people have an extra set of responsibilities to examine how the protection of privilege perpetuates division. We can use these privileges to spark the building of bridges.

I acknowledge that building bridges of deep trust in any diverse setting— be it at work, in the community, or even at home—is a lifelong journey of awareness and capacity building, individually and collectively.[3]

My experience tells me that this journey must begin and be continually supported by actively reaching out to neighbors and fellow travelers, each of you with a beautiful heart and spirit to offer the other.

The good news is that everyone has the capacity to do this ... right now! Today! Tomorrow!

---

3 Appendix A lists some of the resources which have supported my racial equity awareness and capacity journey, and Appendix B is my call to action for forming intentional learning communities across race and class lines, including a framework for the critical areas of learning and practice that are needed to achieve true transformation.

The Magic Combo: Intentionality, Personal Will, and Heart

INTENTIONALITY

You may be saying, "I agree with her, but HOW do I really build better relationships in community life or at work? How do I make new friends?" My answer to you is INTENTIONAL PRACTICES.

Everyone can be intentional. Everyone can try out a new practice. You do this every day with respect to taking care of your home, your car, your pet, or performing at work. And the beauty of relationship-building is that there are no absolute right or wrong answers. We are all action learners. No matter how experienced we are in doing something, everyone is always bumping into a new obstacle or learning from a past mistake and then translating this experience into a new way of doing something.

To help you get started, or to inspire you to try again, I will describe a few intentional practices you might want to consider. I developed this list with the help of over 50 friends from a range of lived experiences, most of whom have spent time thinking about the art of building relationships, especially with those from different backgrounds.

My hope is that this list and stories to help illustrate or explain stimulate you to take a next step.

I also invite you to teach me your lessons learned and your intentional practices. I welcome an ongoing exchange about how to cultivate new friends in this ever-changing world we live in.[4]

Yep! That's what I am thinking.

4   www.startwiththeheartbooks.com; www.trustedspacepartners.com

PERSONAL WILL AND HEART

Before summarizing this list, I want to say a word about the importance of personal will and acting from your heart first.

You already know that a positive spirit will make an encounter with someone go better. If you are like me, you might try to make yourself feel positive. Yet if the feelings aren't there, they just aren't there.

But I have discovered that the very act of making an intentional plan, committing to it, and then having a new experience on which to reflect, makes me feel better and increases my ability to be positive.

So, please do not wait until you have a positive spirit to try out these practices. I think you will discover an emerging shift in attitude and spirit as you take one step and then the next one and the next one. You will see me name a specific attitude shift that emerges in the use of each practice and that supports me in doing better the next time. I hope by naming my attitude shifts, it helps you name and claim your unique shifts.

Don't believe me. Try these practices yourself to see if you agree!

I believe we have two (or more) basic selves: a heart-powered self and an ego-powered self. Our heart-powered self is brave and generous. Our ego-powered self is afraid and protective.

The more we act from our heart and not our mind or ego, the more likely we can find the courage to take a step towards making new or deeper connections. Heart-driven connection also helps us truly listen and receive what the person is saying or offering. It helps us suspend those natural judgments that pop up and quiet the fears rumbling around in our bodies about the need to look or act a certain way.

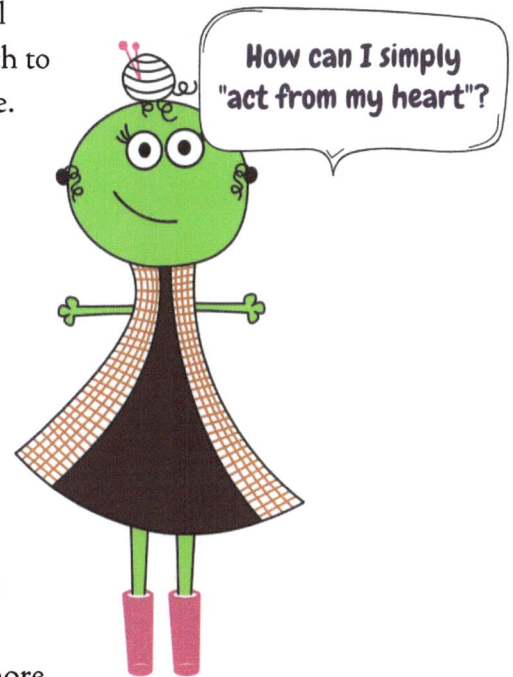

How can I simply "act from my heart"?

THE MAGIC COMBO: INTENTIONALITY, PERSONAL WILL, AND HEART

7

The amazing thing is that heart-driven action often works like a mirror and encourages the person with whom we are connecting to be more heart-centered, or at least a little less afraid or defensive.[5]

Of course, I know that heart-driven action from me doesn't always spark heart-driven action from another. But in the moments when I experience someone acting or talking from a self-protective place, it helps me to remember that we all have two selves (or more), and we all have moments of retreating to ego-driven action or reaction.

I can hear you asking, "How can I simply act from my heart?" The answer is that everyone has their own way of figuring this out. I will share my method, which of course is not foolproof.

I begin most every day with a short time of contemplation, thinking about the people I will meet and reading something that reminds me that love is infinite, available to me at any time.

I have created a fictional person image for my heart self and another for my ego self. They are very different from each other in appearance and personality. When I sense my mind or ego taking over, I am usually afraid or angry. I try to visualize an attic room in my brain where I help this ego self go to bed for a nap. Then I welcome my heart self to sit on a lovely porch (and in a comfortable rocker) outside the bedroom where the ego self is taking a nap.

Visualization can be a powerful practice. For me, the key is to not overthink it. Go with what pops up for you.

• What does your ego self look like ? Where might they retreat?

• What does your heart self look like? Where might they become more present?

5   There is a body of science around the role of mirror neurons in supporting observational learning. See Sandra Blakeslee's *New York Times* article, "Cells that Read Minds."

There are many times when I forget to use this practice, but it helps me tremendously when I do.

There are so many other resources to consult for heart-centered practices. At the time of writing this book, I was consulting Brene Brown's *Atlas of the Heart*, bell hook's All About Love and Barbara Frederickson's *Love 2.0*.

Most important to remember as you read further is that I am providing a framework you can use to expand upon and/or create new practices. Remember, I want to learn from you too!

Everyone Has the Power to Connect

THREE REASONS YOU ARE READY TO CONNECT

1. You are hard-wired for connection

Neuroscientists have discovered that the default network of neurotransmitters in our brains is thinking about and planning for connections with others. One of these scientists, Dr. Matthew Lieberman, told *Scientific American*, "Evolution has placed a bet that the best thing for our brain to do in any spare moment is to get ready to see the world socially . . . We are built to be social creatures." (Cook) This means we are constantly planning for our next meeting or moment of connection. Dr. Vivek Murphy, in his book *Together. The Healing Power of Human Connection in a Sometimes Lonely World*, says that even if we do not realize it—even if we think of ourselves as introverted—we spend the majority of our time thinking about other people.

2. You have a unique kernel of power to offer

One of my mentors, Kaleel Jamison, argues that on the one hand, as human beings, we are alike in many fundamental ways but on the other hand, no two people are truly alike. In *The Nibble Theory and the Kernel of Power, A Book about Leadership, Self-empowerment, and Personal Growth*, she says, "You are unique and I am unique. This is an awesome paradox. And a great mystery." She tells the story of a wise teacher who focused only on helping each child discover the one thing she or he could do well. And, with that as a pivot to give them confidence and a feeling of self-worth, they could do other things, things they never thought they could do.

In passing on this wisdom, Kaleel offers a simple set of prompts and steps for discovering your unique kernel of power. At the age of 44, I found these prompts helped me name and claim my kernel of power and understand that everyone I meet has a unique kernel of power to offer me.

I never got to meet Kaleel before she passed away in 1985, but I have read her book over 100 times and given it to at least that many people for them to read. Her thoughts and book inspired me to write this book. After my struggles in helping lead community change efforts grounded in traditional "positional power analysis," Kaleel helped me see and commit to a form of power sharing that is transformative and offers hope for a better world. Kaleel's work continues through the consulting firm she founded, The Kaleel Jamison Consulting Group, Inc.

I hope you will read both Kaleel's book and this one as companions. I hope you will find a few close friends or work colleagues with whom to try out the practice of naming and claiming your unique kernel of power. I guarantee these two steps will help you in following through with success on these ten relationship-building practices.

Kaleel is quite clear. Our unique kernels of power are not in competition with each other. For Kaleel, power is personal, not positional. When we share our personal power, it only grows and grows infinitely. There is no limit to what we can do and accomplish when we practice our interdependence and share our power.

3. *You have prior successes to draw upon.*

Think of times when you have built a positive relationship with another person. Identify these prior successes and the actions that led to the relationship. It doesn't matter whether you initiated the relationship or not; you can reflect on both the action steps you took and those of the other person And then step back to feel good, pat yourself on your back, and hold this in your back pocket or deep in your heart, as you step out to connect in ways that feel scary and new. You know how to do this!

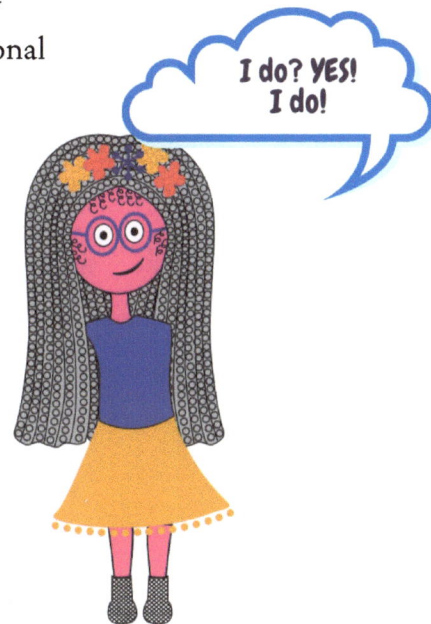

I do? YES! I do!

Accepting the Challenge of Our Differences

My experience in building relationships across lines of difference, particularly those of race and class, has taught me to be in a constant state of intentional awareness building. Efforts to build diverse relationships must be undergirded by a lifelong educational journey, one that focuses on the origin and impacts of systemic racism, imperialism, and capitalism. We must examine how our own behaviors and our community perpetuate these things. I provide a list of resources in Appendix A that continue to help me on my journey.

There are four specific areas of intentional awareness building to highlight. They will be your life vest as you navigate the waters of cross-race and cross-class relationships.

1. Understand Your Filters and Suspend Judgment

Everyone has biases. Over a lifetime, you and every other human being compile a mental database of judgments, beliefs, and prejudices. You draw on this resource to make virtually every decision. But you usually won't know you're checking in with your hidden biases because this database is stored in your unconscious mind. It filters your decisions beyond your awareness.

As a result, we reach conclusions about other people that are simply incorrect. Not only do we miss opportunities to build a relationship, but we also misinterpret reactions to our efforts when reaching out to someone new. I have a very close friend and colleague who is Black and grew up in a northern, urban environment. When I first met him, I found him to be reserved and on the cool side. As a white woman from the South who can come on as too friendly and open, I made the assumption that he didn't like me and would not enjoy working with me. I was incorrect. And gratefully, the circumstances of our working partnership over time revealed my mistaken

assumption. We have gone on to work closely together for nearly ten years, and I consider him one of my most trusted friends.

In these moments of meeting someone new, it helps to pause, step back, and examine these judgments or assumptions as objectively as possible, perhaps with the help of a supportive friend. This does not mean laying your assumptions aside. It means exploring them from different angles. One resource very helpful to me is Howard Ross's book, *Everyday Bias: Identifying and Navigating Unconscious Judgments in Our Daily Lives*.

2. Try Out Empathetic and Generative Listening

You may be aware of active listening, which is listening well enough to provide feedback or a response that demonstrates that we heard what a person said. Some refer to active listening as factual or object-focused listening. For example, if you were listening to someone who says, "I might not go to the party tonight. I had a really bad day at work." You might say, "I hate it when I have a bad day at work".

Empathetic listening moves you one step further, trying to understand how the other person feels. It requires an open heart so that you are connecting with another person from within. Listening with an open heart means we forget about our agenda and begin to see how the world appears through someone else's eyes. In the example above, you might say "I am sorry about your bad day. Tell me more about what happened and how you are feeling."

While I love this idea—seeing the world through someone else's eyes— I also know that as a white person with considerable privilege, I will never be able to fully see the world from the eyes of a person of color or a person who struggles with poverty.

I like the idea of generative listening, which requires an open will to pause long enough to discover how the person you are listening to is calling you to a different, better way of being (Kaeufer and Scharmer.). Every time I connect with a new person, especially someone from a different background, I am presented with the opportunity to act and think differently and pursue a pathway with this person and others, a chance I was not previously aware of. I find that holding onto the idea of an open heart and an open will—even when hard to practice—helps me ride the bumpy waters of relationship building across lines of difference. To continue with the example above, perhaps you ask some follow-up questions once the person describes what happened and any associated feelings, like, "Tell me more about why you are so frustrated"? Or, perhaps you share a similar incident that happened to you at work, while noting that your backgrounds are different and you are interested in learning more about his source of frustration, guessing that it is different than yours.

3. Practice Consistent Kindness

Being kind to others is a simple aspiration that can be hard to practice. As you approach a new moment of connection with someone of a different background, keep in mind two universal truths.

The first universal truth is that most of us approach this new relationship with fear and even distrust. If I am scared or uncomfortable, I may forget my quest to be kind.

The second universal truth is that most of us greatly appreciate it when a person is kindhearted and offers this kindness repeatedly, with no expectation of reciprocity.

If we can make it a practice to remember and accept both truths, we will discover over time greater understanding and patience for folks who cannot offer us kindness in return. And we will find new reserves of patience to continue being kind. As time marches on, this consistent and patient presence will often lead to a fresh opening for connection and relationship building.

4. Let Go of Some

In my long pursuit of building relationships across lines of difference, I have encountered people who were not interested or unable to pursue a relationship with me. Many of the people I interviewed shared this experience too.

Please hold on to this honest acknowledgment and do not be discouraged. Do not give up on your broader quest to build a diverse network of lasting relationships, even when a particular person doesn't respond to your invitations or even when a person flat-out tells you that they are not interested in spending time with you.

You are a beautiful, unique human being with your own kernel of power, and there are many people out there ready to share their kernels of power with you.

Now, let's get going!

Cultivating New Relationships

1 Show up with a Curious Heart

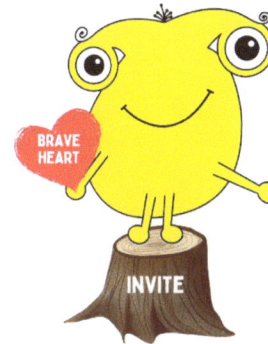

2 Invite with a Brave Heart

3 Persist with a Patient Heart

4 Initiate with a Creative Heart

5 Treasure Hunt with an Open Heart

CURIOUS HEART

SHOW UP

BRAVE HEART

INVITE

PATIENT HEART

PERSIST

CREATIVE HEART

INITIATE

OPEN HEART

TREASURE HUNT

PRACTICE ONE

Show Up with a Curious Heart

FINDING SPACES THAT SUPPORT CONNECTION

You may have heard that famous quote, "Showing up is 80% of life" (Braudy). I fully endorse this bit of wisdom, but believe it needs to go a bit further to say, "Showing up in positive spaces with my best self is 80% of life."

I have witnessed many people decide to become more involved in their local community and show up at a neighborhood association meeting, only to discover that the gathering feels negative and unwelcoming. I believe this type of mismatch moment also happens to new parents at a PTA meeting or new participants in a sports league. The list of well-intended efforts leading to less than positive results go on and on.

My best advice for someone ready to begin showing up more is to do a little thinking and research to determine which kinds of spaces connect to your own affinities and whether the organizers are likely to welcome new faces.

A friend acknowledged:

> It is hard for me to connect with people on my own; one strategy is that I join a new activity, and if someone eventually reaches out to me in this setting, then I lean in to participate. For example, I liked volleyball growing up. So a few years ago, I found a volleyball team to join and started going. At first, I felt intimidated—everyone was from a different neighborhood, more fit, more well off. Finally, one person invited me to the weekly gathering of the team at a local pub. I made a point of showing up consistently. This led to me making some really good friends. I then used the team and these gatherings to invite other people in, as a way of building a relationship with them and introducing them to my volleyball friends.

A strategy that I use when I am in a space unfamiliar to me is to try to sit next to a person or stand near someone who seems nice or more open than others. You can always tell who these folks are: they make eye contact or have a slight smile on their face as others pass by. Then, at a break or when the function is over, I introduce myself and ask a few easy questions such as, "Where do you live? Did you grow up here? What brought you out tonight?"

An acquaintance shared with me her strategy for getting to know a person active in her community circles. She visited the church where this person led the children's story time and heard her suggesting some books to read to the children; afterward, she emailed her and asked for more info and ordered a few of the books. Then after reading them, she checked back in with her acquaintance and referenced one of the books that were meaningful to her. She asked her to meet for coffee to talk about that book. They discovered many similarities over coffee, including the challenges of single parenthood. Now they are frequent guests in each other's homes.

I personally love the strategy of showing up in a space that another person has invited you to or told you about, as a way of affirming them and communicating that you are genuinely interested in getting to know them better. I was recently invited to a large family birthday party for the elderly father of an acquaintance. I genuinely wanted to learn about her family and to let her know that I appreciated the invite. I was a bit nervous because I didn't know anyone and my acquaintance was very busy with food preparation. I did introduce myself to a few people, but I mostly enjoyed taking in the whole wonderful scene. The best part was getting together with my new friend after the party, and listening to the stories flowing from the party, most of which I could make a direct connection with a scene I witnessed.

Tips at a Glance

- It is natural to be worried about what others will think about us. It is also natural to be curious and to want to learn something new. Being curious will help shift the focus from worries and fears about what others may think.

- Some kinds of curiosity can feel judgmental or nosy, and lead to less than positive results; Try to think about a more generous kind of curiosity, a heart-driven kind, where you are open to learning something that will help you be a better person.

- An example of a kind of curiosity that can feel nosy when just getting to know a person might be asking questions about a person's family relationships. Instead, think about your genuine desire to learn about something that is lower stakes, such as places where you have never lived, and ask questions about where a person grew up such as favorite places he or she remembers from the neighborhood.

CURIOUS HEART

SHOW UP

Action and Reflection Prompts

♥ How can I learn more about possible new gathering moments or spaces to check out and meet new people? Once I have a few ideas, which one will I check out first?

♥ What do I need to do to bring my best self?

♥ What did I learn from taking these steps? What next steps will I take?

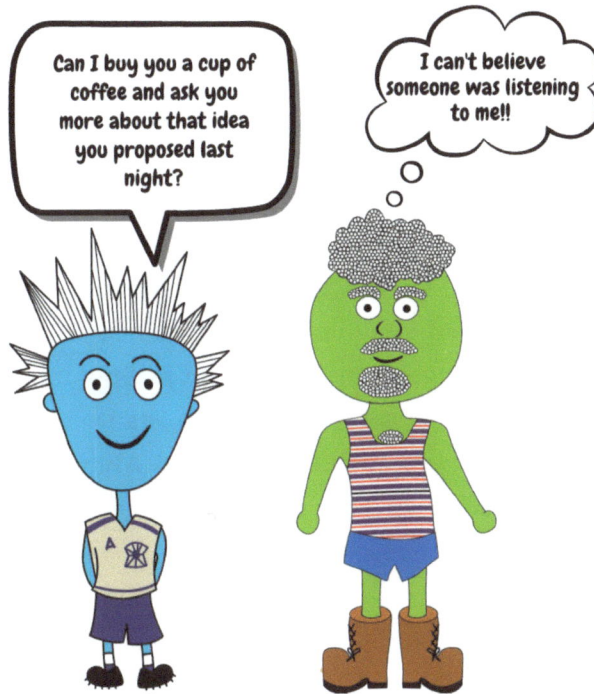

PRACTICE TWO

Invite with a Brave Heart

TAKING THE FIRST STEP TO CONNECT

I believe—and many of those I interviewed agreed—that the single most important practice for relationship building is to invite someone to do something specific.

Do not sit back and wait. More times than not, the person will thank you for taking the initiative and will acknowledge their own fears in this regard.

One friend shared that she is more likely to say yes to an invitation if it is specific in terms of date and time and proposes something that she likes to do. In fact, when she is interested in building a relationship with someone, she actively looks for events or activities that seem to be a good match for that person, even if it isn't something at the top of her list.

> *I heard you say that you have lived here a long time; could you walk with me and tell me more about the neighborhood?*

Another person emphasized the importance of small, easy-to-do steps, like sharing a cup of coffee or taking a walk. When he is feeling a little uncomfortable reaching out to a particular person, he may invite a group of people to do something, like go bowling, see a movie, or ride bikes. Organizing a group outing takes the pressure off and creates a more natural setting in which to begin to get to know a particular person.

I have learned to follow up when someone else makes a connection between me and a third person. It almost always leads to discovering a new friend or acquaintance that enriches my life in a way that I could not have predicted. And, when someone else invites me to go somewhere or to do something, I try very hard to always say yes. Many of those I interviewed mentioned this **Just Say Yes** practice too.

One person, who has a wide and very diverse network of relationships, explained that he will frequently ask a new acquaintance for contact information. But unlike many of us who simply file away this info for some unspecified future time, he assumes that by asking for a phone number, it is his responsibility to make the first call. He'll remember to circle back in a few days with a call to say simply that it was nice to meet you or to invite the new friend to meet him for coffee.

I do believe it is important to name the fears underlying the act of reaching out or responding to someone else who reaches out. Probably the most common fear is that of rejection: the possibility that a person might say no or not respond at all. Most of us have had the experience of asking a person to do something and the person has had a conflict. We then ruminate over whether that conflict is real or made up. Several of those I interviewed said that they actively work to not over-interpret or misinterpret a moment like this. I love this practice, and I know how hard it is to call upon in such a moment.

Another fear on the other end of the spectrum is that of too much of a yes! One friend refers to this as the fear of over-involvement. For example, I have had situations where a casual walk or drink with a new acquaintance was interpreted differently than I thought it would be, perhaps as an opening for them to send me personal texts about their problems. In these situations, since I'm just getting to know someone, I can't figure out what the person needs or is asking of me. I confess to feeling nervous about intentions and whether I can or want to meet the unclear expectations they may have.

Two questions I often ask myself in this situation are these: Do I feel safe emotionally? Is there early evidence of reciprocity and mutuality in the relationship?

Then I might reflect: does the person ask about how I am? Does the person offer wisdom in return for mine?

If the answer is no, I may decide to limit how often I reach out or respond, creating a boundary, while also remaining a good neighbor.

Tips at a Glance

You are not alone in feeling afraid; even those who have a lot of social experience admit that they still feel that wave of fear when sending a new text or dialing a new number.

It can help to name our fears out loud, while also stating to yourself, *the vast majority of my fears are completely unfounded.*

It might help to remember a time in our past, maybe even childhood, when we were less fearful and more inclined to initiate spending time with others.

After some intentional thought, it's best to go ahead and just let the heart lead and quiet your mind.

Another idea is to ask a friend to hold you accountable for taking a step to connect. Don't forget to be specific about when and how they should check in with you.

Action and Reflection Prompts

♥ Do you have any current requests for connection that you can just say yes to?

♥ Who in your current communities (at work, your neighborhood, other contexts) seems most open to connection? What do you know about their favorite activities? Can you find a specific activity to invite them to?

♥ Is there someone whom you recently met that you are genuinely interested in getting to know? What is an easy form of connection to propose? Cup of coffee? Walk? Beer at a local brewery?

♥ Who might you ask to provide support and accountability in taking these steps?

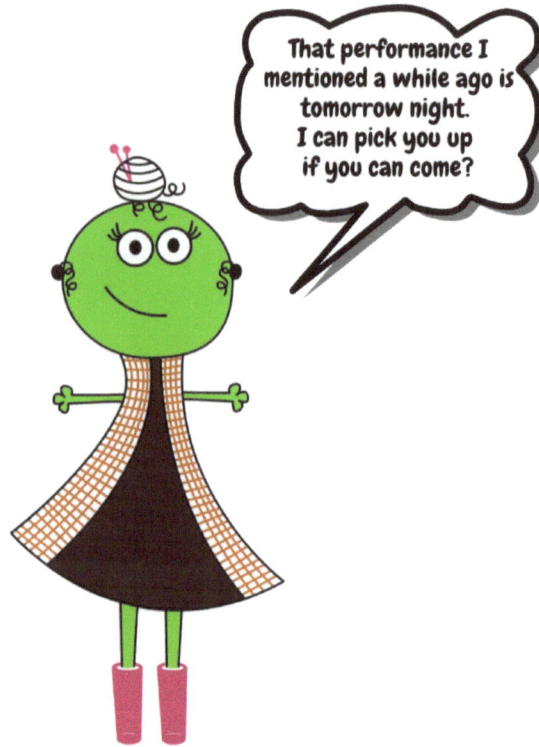

That performance I mentioned a while ago is tomorrow night. I can pick you up if you can come?

PRACTICE THREE

Persist with a Patient Heart

NOT GIVING UP AND/OR KNOWING WHEN TO MOVE ON

As a community organizer, I have spent many years knocking on the doors of strangers to invite them to attend an upcoming community gathering. Most people either say no outright or say yes, but then do not show up. I have learned that most people are afraid to trust the initial invitation as genuine, especially coming from a stranger.

Again, as organizers, we've been taught to live by the principle of **friendly persistence.** So, we always circle back one or two more times, either to try the invite again or to confirm the initial yes.

As we check back in a non-pressured way, we begin to get to know the person a little bit, asking open-ended questions about their lives and perspectives. And, very often, this process of offering multiple invitations, woven in with genuine moments of connection, converts the *no* into a willingness to show up and participate.

I have a lifelong friend—a Latino male considerably younger than me—who teases me about my repeated invitations to him to join a new cross-cultural learning community. He did say yes, and we went on to be full, trusting partners in an effort to reform local schools. We learned so much from each other along the way.

A neighbor, a dogged environmentalist, invites me over and over again to join a newly formed community garden. He has this magical way of letting me know that he genuinely wants me to show up, without making me walk the other way when I see him coming. His magic? He always asks about me and my life first and even remembers to check back in if I share something concerning or a challenge.

It took me a while to begin applying this principle across my life, especially with people I met at church or with my children. I would muster up the energy to invite someone over for dinner or to attend a performance, and then, when they said no, always with lots of explanations, I struggled to not interpret their no as a form of personal rejection. It was hard to ask them again.

This natural feeling of rejection has continued to plague me as a white woman in the sensitive work of seeking out friends of color. In my

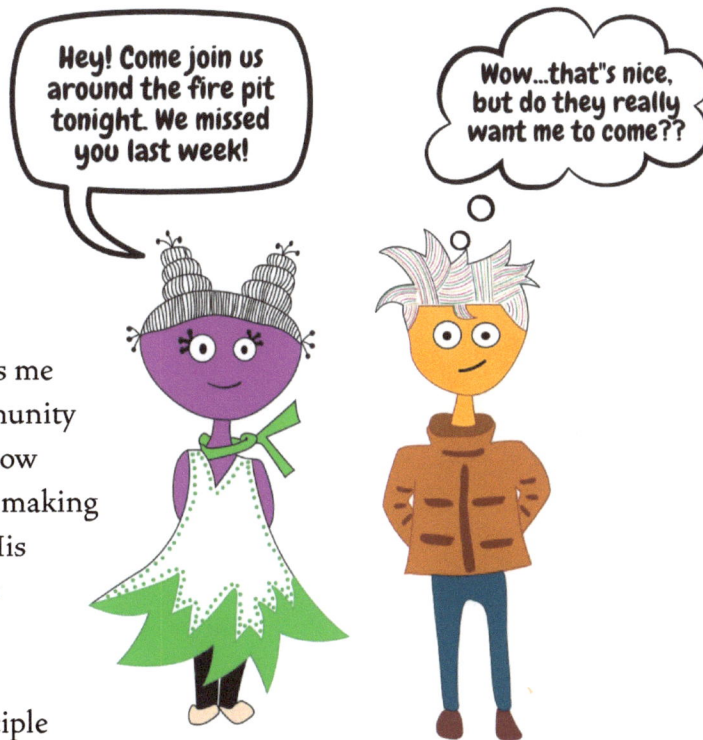

> Hey! Come join us around the fire pit tonight. We missed you last week!

> Wow...that's nice, but do they really want me to come??

PATIENT HEART

PERSIST

Action and Reflection Prompts

❤ Whom might you circle back to in terms of inviting them again to do something with you, even though they did not accept your first invitation? Is there something you learned from previous invitation moments that did not work out, a reflection that you can hold on to in this next moment?

❤ Have you considered the possibility of being more direct and truthful about your intentions, both to demonstrate your authenticity and to help reduce any fears the other person might hold?

❤ Take a moment to write down on a piece of paper all the people whom you care about and who care for you, and hold gratitude for your relationship with them and for yourself as a beautiful human being.

conversations to gather insights for this book, several people spoke about seeking a balance between taking initiative and respecting people's space. They explained that it takes practice to not feel rejected and realize that if you assume the no is about you, you will never reach out to anyone else. In my own experience, I have seen the passage of time or a specific incident open up the possibility of a relationship when I thought it couldn't happen.

Another friend, a Black male, shared a time when he was working hard to build a relationship with a white woman where they both worked in a local elementary school. She kept not accepting his invitations to join in gatherings and parties at his home. He persisted and explained:

> I kept showing up in her spaces and asking for her feedback. I was not afraid of tension and conflict. She had a gift with kids. I wanted to learn from her. Speaking the truth in love to her eventually led to a beautiful friendship.

Tips at a Glance

• Remember that we all live busy and complicated lives and that we are mostly focused on getting through each day.

• You are not alone in misinterpreting a turn down; we all do it on a repeated basis.

• Remember the times you could not or did not say yes.

• It can't hurt to reflect a little when someone resists a connection with you. What can you learn?

• Most importantly, remember that you are a beautiful person, as well as the person with whom you are trying to connect. AND, there are many people in this world who want to connect with you.

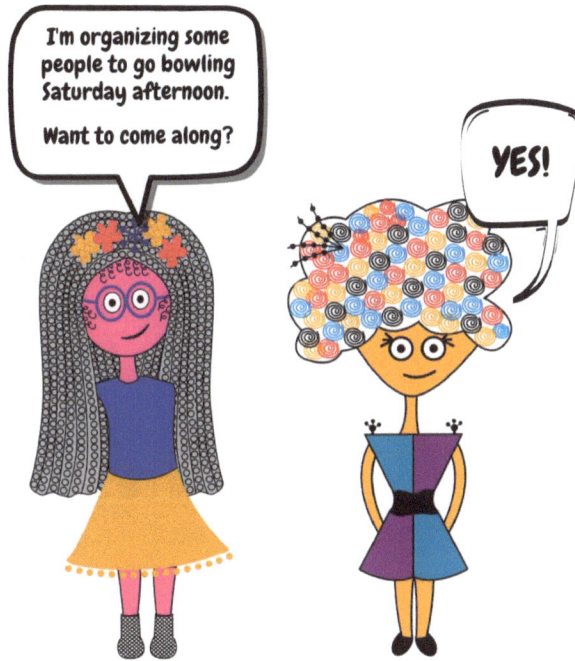

PRACTICE FOUR

Initiate Moments with a Creative Heart

FACILITATING OPPORTUNITIES TO CONNECT

I know in my heart that everyone enjoys having fun with others while it's also true that many people keep to themselves because it is scary or time-consuming to connect with others and to organize fun events. Even with these truths in mind, I find myself repeatedly coming up with a plan to bring people together, and then sitting on the ideas for months, even years. I have been plotting a potluck picnic for my neighborhood for over six years. Seriously!

One way I have overcome this tendency to delay is to lean into creating more spontaneous events that require very little preparation. A joyful moment in this regard was planning several Saturday afternoon gatherings at a local bowling alley, with the help of my life partner, where we sent a text invite to about 20 people only two days ahead of time. Each time, at least half of the folks we invited showed up, which in my book is a success! All we did was reserve the bowling alleys, and I brought some baskets of candy to pass around. But that was it. Otherwise, those attending loved an excuse to eat and drink at the bowling alley.

If you are sitting on a similar idea for a gathering, find a friend or acquaintance to co-initiate the gathering; it helps reduce the fear and it holds you accountable for moving forward with the plans.

A close work colleague and friend, who is Black, decided he wanted to check out pickleball. He found a local group, composed mostly of other Black people, hosting pickleball hours and began showing up on a regular basis. One day, he was chatting with another player, and she mentioned that she wanted to get to know their fellow players but didn't know how. After reflecting that he felt similarly, he decided to propose a lunch gathering for the group via text exchanges. Now the group meets regularly off the court to celebrate each other's birthdays and to mix with other groups, some of which are mostly white. And best of all, everyone is taking turns initiating their gatherings.

One Latina friend shared that she had a co-worker whom she wanted to get to know better. Through conversation she discovered that they both enjoyed creative projects. This gave her impetus to host a holiday card-making party, to which she invited her co-worker and a few others. She shared with me:

> I was a little nervous—she is a white girl—and I worried about judgments she may have about my house. But I forged ahead with the thought in my head—I don't care if someone does not like me. She's going to!

My life partner shared that he works extra hard to listen to new people he meets, especially those who bring a different background or perspective. He went on to say,

I also try to remember that I am an older white man. I don't want to make someone feel uncomfortable. I stay in a casual mode for a long time. While I am not the best initiator, I look for random opportunities to bump into them. I refer to this practice as random intentionality.

Tips at a Glance

• Be sure to use fun moments as a casual time to ask open-ended questions and to listen with your heart!

• We often think that we have no good ideas for gathering others together. If we stay open, ideas often pop up in our minds or land in front of our faces

• Building upon a shared interest is a great place to start. Asking others for ideas can spark your unique imagination.

• Think about others who have a creative heart and imitate these moments; copy their steps, actions, and behaviors.

Action and Reflection Prompts

♥ Make a list of all the activities, events, and places to visit near where you live or work (Concerts, ball games, art exhibits, vendor markets, hikes, games, arcade, etc.)

♥ Which of these ideas are most appealing to you? Which are the easiest to access, logistically and financially? Who can you recruit to co-organize an outing or gathering together?

♥ Who might want to come along with you? Who are you less certain about but can be included in your invitation?

♥ What is the best way to create a group invitation or a one-on-one invitation? (Think about the kind of invitation you would like to receive.)

♥ What are some good open-ended questions to ask during your time together?

I love the way you greet people who pass by on the street. Where did you pick up that practice?

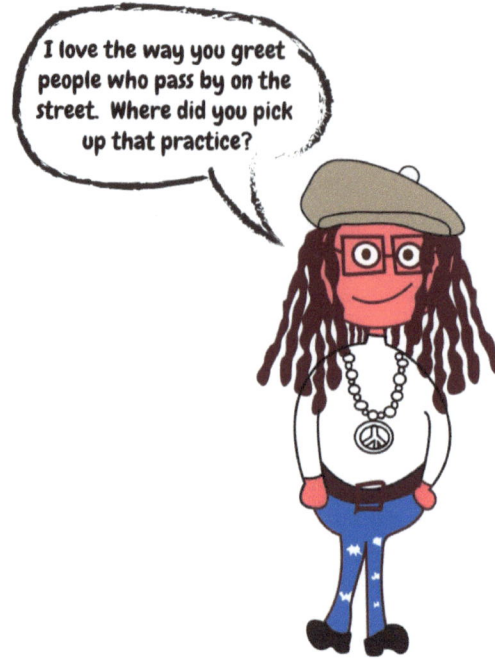

PRACTICE FIVE

Treasure Hunt with an Open Heart

DISCOVERING UNIQUE STORIES AND GIFTS

Every single human being has the potential to bring unique value to the people they know at work or school, the neighbors they live near, and the broader community. Truly, **wisdom is everywhere**!

Sadly, much of this unique value remains hidden by all kinds of fear, assumptions, biases, and even anger. If we are honest with ourselves, most of our relationships remain on the surface or only last a short while, never deepening into genuine belonging, respect, and exchange of unique wisdom.

And if we are really honest, most of our genuine relationships of mutual exchange and respect are with people who have similar backgrounds and cultures. Our lives could be so much richer, and we could solve so many more personal and community problems if we learn how to find and honor each other's unique treasure—treasure rooted in our beautiful diversity and differences.

I believe two simple steps, repeated over and over again, can increase our ability to **find treasure** in others even when fear and uncertainty are present.

First Step: We need to recognize that we each carry a story of the other in our heads, based solely on their appearance, well before any words are exchanged. We are not bad people for this. Society bakes into our unconscious mental maps that are immediately triggered when encountering a new person for the first time.

Second Step: We need to learn how to ask comfortable, open-ended questions over time to slowly uncover a person's true story and unique value. Everyone likes to be listened to. Everyone likes to share some of their life experiences. Briefly sharing your story or a specific personal experience helps encourage another person to do the same.

Consistent and repeated use of these two steps over a period of time will tear down our incorrect assumptions and soften our hearts for all kinds of possible exchanges and connections.

A friend connected me to a nonprofit service provider in his school, someone who immigrated to the US from El Salvador as a teenager and who enjoys many diverse relationships. She told me that her accent always leads to a conversation.

People ask where I am from. I readily share my story. I say — I am an immigrant from El Salvador. I am very proud. I always ask them about their story. Even if they are a white person with little knowledge of their origin story, I discover so much about the many places people are from in the United States.

A few years ago, I got to work alongside a younger white community organizer in a mostly Black neighborhood in Washington, D.C. She became

This pie is yummy!
Do you cook a lot?
What are your specialties?

closely connected to one of the Black residents who was middle-aged and surviving on a very limited income. I asked my colleague what she learned about crossing so many lines of difference to forge a connection with this woman, as well as several others. She said that her key practice is to do lots and lots of listening, without always expecting the same in return. She also believes in checking in with new friends on a regular and random basis, and in being patient with how long it takes to establish an initial foundation of trust. She added,

I always look for something in common or something that gives me safety and comfort to talk about. Getting to know a person's story is a comfortable place to begin for me.

I am fortunate to know several younger men working to build a network of what they refer to as "young creatives," people in their twenties and thirties who are working to develop their talents and gifts in ways that benefit the community. Their go-to practice for finding and knowing people better, both their stories and their gifts, is to create non-transactional spaces, like Weekly Taco Night and Creative Saturdays to which they can invite new people. They say that the two most important ingredients of these intentional spaces are rituals (like story-sharing prompts or check-in questions) and consistency (setting a regular schedule and sticking to it).

One of my favorite **wisdom-is-everywhere** stories is when a close friend and I started a conversation circle with some folks to practice English and Spanish together. We recruited several native Spanish speakers (complete strangers to us) from a food pantry line at our church. Our diverse circle of 10 people met every Monday night for almost a year. We spent a lot of time sharing our life stories with each other, while we also practiced Spanish and English. Of course, every single person brought unique gifts to teach the other, beyond our mutual language support.

One relationship we forged was with a man who mowed and tended lawns. When he learned that we were working to help start community-based cooperatives in our town, he completely jumped in with his wide network of other landscapers and his unique understanding of shared finances. Two years later, he became a lead organizer of a highly successful financial credit cooperative, all led by its members who are contractors of various backgrounds in our community.

Tips at a Glance

- Remember that when we meet someone for the first time, we need to consciously suspend any snap judgments that pop up from our unconscious mind and stay open to learning about this person's unique story.

- Everyone has a unique kernel of power to contribute to a community or organization. We need to help each other feel invited and comfortable in sharing our kernels of power.

- Helping a person contribute is better than helping them with a problem.

- Periodic moments of silence are not bad and can support thoughtful reflection and are always better than filling up spaces with mindless chatter.

OPEN HEART

TREASURE HUNT

Action and Reflection Prompt

💗 Reflect on a time when someone asked you a good, open-ended question, one that made you feel seen and one that you enjoyed answering.

💗 How can you use this experience to think of a good question to ask someone else?

💗 How did the conversation go? What did you learn?

💗 As you practice good question asking and listening, what surprises are you encountering? Have you made some assumptions that are incorrect?

💗 What are your reflections about the limitations of a *helping mindset* and how this can inhibit the ability to connect more fully with others and find new wisdom?

💗 What new wisdom are you discovering in these conversations, wisdom that you can both affirm and share with others?

The Quest for Lasting Relationships

These last five practices are offered as tools to help build a network of lasting relationships, a network that provides a sense of belonging, a place to contribute our gifts, and a source of support for managing daily life and pursuing our dreams.

Unless we build networks of lasting relationships with different kinds of people, we cannot achieve a true sense of belonging nor can we find the diverse resources needed to build a better life and a better world.

What do we mean by lasting relationships? We each have our own way of defining this. I do better in this world when I know that there are others in my community and my life who think about me from time to time, who are interested in what I do and say (and sometimes challenge me!), and who are happy to hear from me, even when I am calling to ask for help. I believe we are hard-wired to need a significant group of people who meet these criteria, even though many profess otherwise and too many live without such a network.[6]

Not every person we meet and get to know will become a lasting relationship in our lives. It is important to accept this fact and to acknowledge that we cannot sustain lasting relationships with every new person we get to know.

No matter what transpires, short-term relationships always bring us a new window to the world and a lesson to hold on to moving forward. And this applies to both parties. So, short-term relationships are good and a natural part of living a full life.

---

6   There are many resources on the growing epidemic of loneliness. I recommend Vivek H. Murthy's book, *Together: The Healing Power of Human Connection in a Sometimes Lonely World* as a great starting point and summary of other experts and their research.

Nuturing Lasting Relationships

10 Share Power with an Active Heart

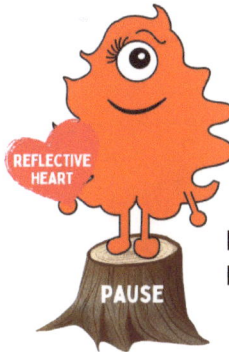

(ACTIVE HEART)
(SHARE POWER)

6 Pause with a Reflective Heart

(REFLECTIVE HEART)
(PAUSE)

7 Check-in with an Attentive Heart

(ATTENTIVE HEART)
(CHECK-IN)

9 Ride the Roller Coaster with a Forgiving Heart

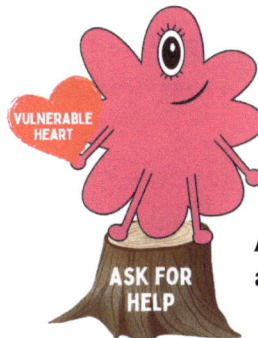

(FORGIVING HEART)
(RIDE THE ROLLER COASTER)

8 Ask for Help with a Vulnerable Heart

(VULNERABLE HEART)
(ASK FOR HELP)

PRACTICE SIX

Pause with a Reflective Heart

TAKING TIME TO LEARN AND CHANGE

I hope that these practices feel empowering to you. I acknowledge that the process of building relationships, especially relationships across lines of difference, is not easy or natural. If it was, there would be no need for books like this one.

The pathway towards a network of relationships is available to everyone, with some intentionality and with a reflective heart

What does it mean to be intentional? What does it mean to have a reflective heart?

One very wise person whom I interviewed talked about our Western/ European culture's need to get to the goal . . . to see the outcome clearly and the strategy to get there. She referred to this as the fix-it mentality or the goal-oriented culture. I admit to being far too goal-oriented. How about you?

She went on to explain that many other cultures are more process-oriented and support taking time for reflection. Her technique for bridging cultures is to slow down and pause. She explained:

> I know for myself whenever I can bring enough intention to pause no matter what it is I am facing or doing, something new and/or unseen opens up. Or when I can let go of the outcome, there is something valuable that comes from the plain old process.

The first five practices in this book focus mostly on initiating new relationships and moving from introduction to a place of greater knowing, understanding, and appreciation for a particular person. In pausing to reflect on a particular relationship, be it a newly forming or a pre-existing one, try asking yourself some questions such as these:

- What am I learning from this exchange?
- What do I value about this person?
- Am I authentically curious to learn more?
- Do they seem to value and have an authentic curiosity about me?
- Am I my best self when I am around them?
- Do I seem to bring out their best self?

As you reflect, be sure to sit with an honest but soft heart. Don't be led by those natural voices of judgment that pop up, either with respect to the person whom you are in a relationship with or about yourself. Return to the introduction in this book, where I identified the strong filters and unconscious biases that we all have and must actively work to overcome. But also remind yourself that we are hard-wired to connect with one another and that you always carry your own kernel of power and life experiences in making connections with others.

Action and Reflection Prompts

♥ Make a list of people who are in your current network of lasting relationships.

♥ Periodically review the list and ask:

What am I learning from them?

What do I value about them?

Am I bringing my best self to our relationship?

This active, internal struggle is the process of pausing with a reflective heart. When you feel your heart shutting down because of fear, frustration, or even anger, try to find someone who is on a similar quest as yours, tell them about your reflection process and be honest about your feelings. Ask them about their process, feelings and lessons learned. When I think back on my own journey, I know that without safe spaces to share and learn from others who share in my quest for a diverse network of relationships, I would have given up long ago.

One other reflection practice I find useful is to sit and make a list several times a year of those people I have or want to have a lasting relationship with. I do not dwell on this list or look at it very often, but the act of writing the list down helps me remember how special these people are to me and keeps them close in my heart, as I go about my daily life. And it spurs me on to keep reaching out to people who bring me a different perspective or life experience.

Tips at a Glance

- Slowing down to let go of your specific goals and pursuits from time to time will open space for other possibilities to emerge.

- Imagine your heart softening and your mind letting go of previous judgments and fears. I try to think of a place that is soothing to me—like sitting with my feet in a cold babbling brook on a hot day—to regroup and find my heart.

- Constantly review the presence of unconscious bias and filters and ask if any of these have been getting in the way.

- Find someone you trust and who is on a similar quest to talk about your feelings and reflections.

PRACTICE SEVEN

Check In with an Attentive Heart

REMEMBERING AND THINKING OF OTHERS

So, how do we cultivate these kinds of trusting and interdependent relationships, once we know someone a little bit and we sense that they are interested in a lasting relationship?

Almost every single person I interviewed said that random check-ins with their close friends are the most important way to both cultivate and preserve a relationship over time. Likewise, almost everyone spoke about the importance of remembering something specific to ask about or to refer to when you do check-in. Several went on to suggest that when checking in on a friend, sharing something specific about your own life is a good way to make them feel comfortable sharing with you.

A few people referred to their practice of writing cards, both randomly and at key moments in the year or to express gratitude for something specific. One person suggested that kind gestures like a handwritten note need to flow out of a genuine moment and should not feel obligatory. She offered this example.

> I knew a person who was very upset about losing her dog. A few weeks later, I sent a card to her letting her know that I was thinking about her. She told me that my card meant a lot to her. I remember her comment as an extra push to write others a card in a similar moment.

One interesting and evolving conversation among those I know is how we make unplanned phone calls. Societal norms have shifted in this regard, but I still use this practice with a core group of about ten good friends, my family, and when I am in the process of cultivating a very new friend.

One friend talked about her love of phone calls. She said:

> I can tell so much more about how my friend is really doing by hearing their voice. But, in truth, I am now afraid to even cold call my own family members.

One thing I do when cold calling a friend or family member is immediately say - when they answer – *Hi! I know I am calling out of the clear blue, and you may not have time to talk right now, but I just had a minute and wanted to hear your voice and find a time to schedule a longer phone call. I am excited to catch up with you.*

One person, an African American man, said that his key practice for keeping friends close and cultivated is texting to check in.

I use my text history to remind myself to do this, periodically scrolling back through to see if I have not been in touch in a while and then reaching out. I once went to an equity conference and started chatting with a woman of Hispanic background. We discovered our common love of cooking and baking. We have kept in touch by text ever since, mostly around sharing our common interests. It did lead to a relationship with someone who is very different from me.

Another friend, when asked about keeping up with good friends, said she looks to find shared experiences, like going to a play, hosting a game night, and sharing a new kind of food. She says,

> I do not plan ahead. This needs to be spontaneous for me to do it. Some people are afraid of being rejected; but by making it spontaneous, I don't have to worry about this as much.

Tips at a Glance

• We all like to be seen and heard, and mostly feel like we are not. Stay aware of this truth when you are hesitant to reach out to a friend or family member. Use it as the extra impetus you need to send a text or make a phone call.

• The difference between attentive and nosy is subtle but important. For example, try to use open-ended questions like "How are you feeling?" or "How did it go?" and accept the response without pressing for more details.

• Acknowledgment of a specific situation or feeling is a powerful tool.

• Learning the art of careful observation, while quieting the chatter of our own minds, will give you access to your attentive heart.

ATTENTIVE HEART

CHECK-IN

Action and Reflection Prompts

❤ Who is someone you want to check in with today? How will you do it and what will you ask?

❤ Is there a spontaneous event or moment you can invite a few friends to in the next few days? Whom will you invite and how?

❤ As you look back on your text history or a list of your friends, do you remember anything about their current life circumstances that might prompt a phone call or a thoughtful card in the mail?

PRACTICE EIGHT

Ask for Help with a Vulnerable Heart

EXCHANGING STORIES AND MUTUAL SUPPORT

I was raised in a household where the Good Samaritan story from the New Testament was the driving vision of how we were supposed to show up in life. This core belief of serving others was combined with an equally strong cultural message that we are never to burden another with our own selfish needs. In short, you should always help others, but you should never ask for help.

How messed up is this as a way of living? It completely undermines and disregards the universal truth that wisdom is everywhere. In fact, the underlying assumption of my Christian upbringing is that I am better than you and therefore you need me, but I could not possibly need you.

It took many years to undo the impact of this deeply ingrained message on my ability to build authentic relationships, especially relationships across lines of difference. I am still working on it. I began to shift when I realized that my best relationships with other people grew out of shared moments where someone else, or some process, prompted me to be more vulnerable, typically in a group setting.

In one intense community organizing moment, our team committed to doing 10,000 door knocks during the 2008 economic recession, to check in on people and to connect them to public/private resources, (i.e.), to help them. We agreed to this quest, knowing that the excuse to door knock gave us a chance to invite newcomers into our growing community network and our campaign for long-term systemic change.

The process of making genuine connections with neighbors across a diverse range of backgrounds, where in any given apartment complex, we encountered as many as 12 different ethnicities and language groups, was more difficult than first realized. We discovered that if we immediately revealed something that our group needed—a need that the neighbor might be able to provide—that person was more likely to accept our invitation. For example, we were always looking for people with different language abilities, social media skills, party planning expertise, or the ability to plan activities for kids. People feel better when they are helping versus when they are being helped.

A few years later, a younger friend from a very different background than mine told me that I was good at asking others to be vulnerable but not so good at asking for help in my life. Her honest feedback woke me up. Over time, I have improved at revealing my personal stresses and challenges and receiving with grace what this friend and others offer me. I am forever grateful that my friend had the courage to provide me feedback and did it in a way that felt loving and not judgmental.

Another person who came to the United States from El Salvador as a young teen shared a story about the power of vulnerability. She decided to take a guitar class as an elective, even before she could speak much English. She shared this:

> I was the only Latino in the class. It was the first time I spoke English in a mixed setting. I asked this white guy to help me. We became friends, mostly around helping each other with the guitar. We have stayed friends through his time in the military, and then when we were both at the local community college, we still met up for coffee.

Do you know anyone who is good at dealing with the cable company? I've got to lower my monthly bill!

Yes. I do. My next door neighbor has helped several of us with cable company bills. I'll introduce you to her.

Because most of us struggle to express vulnerability in a world dominated by the ethos of independence, one idea is to build practices of mutual exchange into our work and community lives. I love the story of my friend who was relatively new to a community and decided to hold a big sleepover for women in her neighborhood. She revealed on Facebook that she didn't get to have the kinds of sleepovers portrayed on TV and invited her female Facebook friends to the sleepover. Her goal was simply to enjoy fellowship and good food with women.

Thirty women accepted, and during the evening (not everyone slept over), she held a wisdom circle. She had some questions in a bowl, and everyone picked a question to answer. She asked everyone to simply listen and not respond unless it was their turn. In reflecting later, my friend shared that this one-time evening exchange led to many special relationships across age, class, and race and did not obligate people to make relationships if they did not want to.

Another practice to consider is something my partner and I call **the marketplace practice.** It is easy to facilitate. At the end of a team meeting, a dinner party, or any gathering, everyone gets a chance to make a simple request or offer, something that one or two people can fulfill without a huge expenditure of time or effort. Some of my favorite examples of matches made between the various requests and offers are: a phone conversation about parenting teenage girls, sharing tips for using coupons successfully, or providing a ride to the grocery store on a regular basis.

Tips at a Glance

- People feel better when they are helping versus when they are being helped. If you always are the one serving or helping, you risk dominating or overpowering a relationship.

- The more specific a request is, the better. Instead of, *I need help painting my house,* you might try *something like I am looking for 3 friends to help paint my living room on Saturday, July 30.* This helps a potential giver determine whether they can assist.

- Following through on an offer to help affirms the person and opens up new possibilities for getting to know each other.

- The more we reveal our humanity, the more chance we have of finding those who have similar struggles or can empathize.

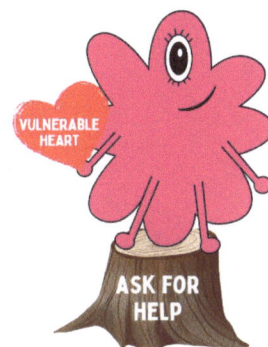

Action and Reflection Prompts

❤ Are you currently involved in a relationship where you are the helper? Is there an authentic opening for you to seek support or even a small favor from this person?

❤ In what area of your life are you feeling the most challenged or afraid or alone? Who might have gone through a similar moment or might have specific wisdom to offer you? What is your plan for reaching out to them?

❤ How can you be more intentional in revealing your fears and doubts in your daily conversations with friends, co-workers, neighbors and family, in a way which invites support without being overwhelming?

❤ What ideas do you have for trying out the **marketplace practice** where you work or in your community life?

PRACTICE NINE

Ride the Roller Coaster with a Forgiving Heart

LEARNING AND GROWING

As intentional people in pursuit of lasting relationships, we must respect others and realize that our intentions at any moment do not necessarily match up with another person's. And we all have good days and bad days, positive moods and negative moods. Sometimes, reaching out, forming, or deepening a friendship can feel like a roller coaster ride. Sometimes it is fun and easy. Sometimes it is fraught with fear and frustration. And the process of cultivating a friend can come to a complete standstill and even move backward.

The image of a roller coaster helps me remember this up-and-down feeling and accept that it is a real condition out of my control. Of course, if the loops and drops never lessen with a particular person, it may be time to move on or create a boundary. In my current life, I have two close friends whom I think, but I do not know for sure, have different intentions about our relationship. They are not initiating contact as much as I am, and when we connect, I feel greater distance than in our past exchanges. I have one acquaintance I've tried for several years to build a closer relationship with, and she seems happy to hear from me but not as interested in spending time together. While these situations don't feel good, and I know I need to do something to either let go of or resolve the uneasy feelings, I am a bit frozen, letting each day go by with no additional action.

Below, I offer five specific practices to try out, depending on the circumstances, to ease the scary sensations that come along with all relationship building. As I offer these to you, I know that I need to muster up the courage to use these practices in my life with these beautiful people I love.

But first, I want to explicitly name and revisit the specific fear and frustration that I, and most others I know, experience when cultivating friends of a different race or culture and friends who live in different economic situations. To be honest, of the two situations I named above, both friends are people of color, and in my ruminations about what to do and what to say, I know my whiteness creates an extra layer of fear to unpack, understand, and overcome.

I asked everyone I interviewed for one critical insight they have gained from the pain and joy of their efforts to cross differences. Here are a few to hold on to:

> "I put myself in their shoes as much as possible and ask: What would make me comfortable?"

"I try to understand my filters and avoid jumping to conclusions."

"I remind myself that I cannot ever fully understand another person's dynamics and upbringing."

"I try to be intentional in not taking up too much space as a white man."

"I find that the key is to keep assessing and respecting boundaries."

"I work to remain genuine in seeing people as people, and I try to exercise patience, being okay with limited reciprocity."

"When I find a connection across lines of difference, I invest in it."

"I try to be honest in acknowledging our differences."

"I think carefully about the questions I ask, making sure they arise from genuine curiosity versus nosiness."

"I try to see the good in people, even in conflict, and to see them more fully than one interaction."

"If a person is guarded, I either go the extra mile to connect or step back and be chill."

"I devote more time to allow me to see a person from different lights; I listen a lot and ask non-judgmental questions."

"I take risks and step out of my comfort zone."

Specific Practices to Ease the Ups and Downs of the Roller-Coaster Ride

EMBRACING AWKWARDNESS

When raising my three children, I repeatedly coached them on the need to let go of or ignore awkward feelings, whether they were pursuing a relationship or addressing a misunderstanding with a friend. When I was their age, I also experienced the pain of feeling awkward, and likely missed or lost some wonderful friendships because of my discomfort.

I only learned the lesson of embracing awkwardness when I was engaging community members in a wide range of settings and accountable to my co-workers. I discovered that the vast majority of people are glad to hear from you, no matter how much time has passed or strange the request. Even with a past interpersonal conflict, many are glad to hear from you. I still get nervous and uncomfortable in many relational moments. But the memory of pushing through to a better place in prior moments helps me muster up the next bit of courage and strength to let myself feel awkward!

I was delighted to recently discover a book by Daniel Pink called *The Power of Regret*, in which he shares stories and research about a similar practice, which he calls "pushing past awkwardness." He highlights stories of relationships that drift apart, for no specific reason, and the drifting creates awkwardness for the two people involved in reaching back out again. In one case, a woman discovers that her long-ago friend is dying of cancer, and because of feelings of awkwardness, the woman waits until it is too late to pick up the phone and connect with her (Pink—).

Don't Take Things Personal

In my interviews for this book, I sought to dig deeper into the hard aspects of building relationships, both initially and when deepening relationships. Many responded that their key strategy is to not over-interpret the response or lack of response.

A very close friend and work colleague says it this way:

> I have learned that most people are pleased that I am reaching out to them, so when I get a less-than-positive response, I don't take it personally.

WHAT DO YOU MEAN – Don't take anything personal?

That is hard! I am a sensitive person.

I confess that I am a very sensitive person, and this practice is extremely hard for me. I worked intentionally on this barrier for years, and only got a breakthrough after reading Don Miguel Ruiz's *The Four Agreements*. He argues that most of us live in our own "dream" or mind and that this dream is governed by a complex set of fear-based agreements with ourselves, causing us to expend a lot of energy in the form of worry and anger and other negative emotions (Ruiz —). He counsels the reader to find the courage to break those agreements that are fear-based and claim our personal power. He offers four simple agreements that come from love and help us conserve energy and even gain extra energy, one of which is "Don't take anything personal" (Ruiz—). He explains, "When we take something personally, we make the assumption that they know what is in our world, and we try to impose our world on their world" (Ruiz —).

Checking In with One Another to Learn

In the early 2000s, while working to build a multi-racial, mixed-income community network in Silver Spring, Maryland, I learned early on how quickly intrapersonal challenges arise in the process of building relationships. Of course, even when working in more homogeneous settings, I knew well the struggle of bringing human beings together towards common goals or even navigating daily life together. During this particular time of intentional network building, I and my community colleagues were fortunate to receive a lot of coaching from a team of skilled people who made their living teaching others how to connect across differences.

With the team's valuable help, we focused on developing everyone's skill at providing and receiving feedback, both to avoid conflict or to transform conflict. Conflict always arises and is a natural phenomenon among human beings. The key takeaway for me from the practice of feedback is to never accuse someone of something, but instead name a feeling that you experienced when the person did something and then ask for the chance to understand the situation better. This approach is grounded in your own true feelings (which no one can challenge) and not on your assessment, which is often incorrect. As a result, I am a big believer in helping everyone become skilled at both providing and receiving feedback. Check out the Center for Creative Leadership's Situation-Behavior-Impact method (SBI ™) of providing effective feedback.

We learned over time how hard it is to put the feedback practice into action, especially in a busy and hectic community setting. We eventually settled on a simpler version called the **Check-in Practice.** It is a simple prompt to remember and use when you are struggling with something that happened with another person.

It goes like this:

> I need to check in with you about [the incident or exchange] and better understand what was going on from your perspective and share my feelings about [the incident or exchange].

One person I interviewed provided a simple check-in story. She got involved in a local church and liked the fact that all the members are tight knit, but also referenced a time when she felt excluded from a particular group inside the church. She decided to check in with one of the people involved, knowing that she was operating on some assumptions that may have not been true. And, in fact, her assumptions were inaccurate, and the process of having an honest, intentional conversation with her church friend helped preserve the friendship and her ability to enjoy this newfound community.

Another friend, a Black male, told me about how the father of one of his son's friends, a white male, reached out and asked for his help in becoming a better man, especially when it comes to issues of race. My friend proposed

the joint reading and discussion of some books, which they did on three occasions. After a while, the son's friend's father stopped responding to texts and calls. At a holiday open house, my friend decided to check in with him and learned that he had felt lectured to during the book discussions. My friend took this to heart and proposed that instead of books and conversations, they enjoy watching games at a sports bar together. This simple but proactive step of checking in preserved the friendship and opened more possibilities for learning and growing together, this time over beer and sports.

Acceptance

You understand by now that intentionality can lead to deeper and more diverse relationships and a greater sense of belonging. However, I do want to fully acknowledge that there are potential relationships and communities where it is better to intentionally accept that they are not available to you or good for you.

As a mother of three daughters, each of whom experienced scary roller-coaster rides in their young adult years, I got pretty good at helping them accept situations that would not produce positive outcomes. And as a white community activist trying to forge collaborations with many different persons of color, I have encountered wonderful folk who did not want to be in a relationship or community with me. Several people I interviewed referenced similar moments where they needed to simply accept and let go.

In these moments, one practice to consider is the reciting of the well-known Serenity Prayer, made famous by Alcoholics Anonymous:

> God, grant me the serenity to accept the things I cannot change, the courage to change the things I can, and the wisdom to know the difference. — *The Serenity Prayer and Me*

Forgiving Heart

Through several painful relationships in my life, I discovered that practicing forgiveness is the best way to let go and not dwell on the conflict and hurtful moments that are inevitable in human connection.

Reading and listening to wise people from the world of spiritual growth and psychology taught me that forgiveness is not the same as forgetting or approving someone's bad act or inaction. Forgiveness is about letting your heart be free of a previous incident or person, so you can be free to live the next moment more fully. It is about taking care of yourself. Living in a place of blame, anger, and even victimhood will negatively impact all aspects of your physical and emotional health.

The practice of forgiveness also opens the possibility to see more fully the person who hurt you and to understand that people can grow and change and that painful relationships can be restored. In one of her many guided meditations on forgiveness, Tara Brach, a well-known psychologist, and teacher of emotional healing, offers this beautiful explanation:

> When we are in the blame mode, we've lost touch with our own greatness of heart. We are not living from the truth of who we are and our full potential. We are seeing a person or a situation from a very small aperture. We can no longer see or access the goodness that may be available.

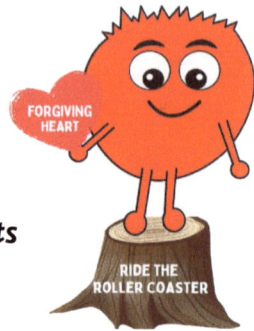

Action and Reflection Prompts

💙 Make a list of your current relationships where you feel uncertain or stuck. Select one or two high priorities off this list. Is there a step you can take to re-engage, even though it may feel awkward or even scary?

💙 Have you recently experienced a difficult moment with a particular person? Do you think checking in with them can help both of you get to a better place? Can you "role play" the check in practice with someone else first?

💙 How does observation of the filters and biases that others operate with, inform you about your filters and biases? Is there someone whom you trust that you can ask for feedback in this regard?

💙 How might you best apply the practice of forgiveness in your life right now?

FORGIVING HEART

RIDE THE ROLLER COASTER

Tips at a Glance

• Push past the awkwardness to connect when you've lost touch with someone.

• In relating with someone, don't take anything personally; your reality is not their reality.

• When a difficult exchange occurs, take time to check in, seeking to learn their perspective first.

• Be willing to accept that there are people who do not want to be in relationship with you. And remember that not everyone in your life is bringing their best selves to your relationship and you may need to create a boundary to protect yourself.

• Study and try the practice of forgiveness to free up your heart from blame and hurt.

PRACTICE TEN

Share Power with an Active Heart

GIVING AND RECEIVING GIFTS FOR THE GREATER GOOD

One of the most challenging lines of difference that we all must cross when we are intentionally building a diverse network of relationships is that of positional power.

Positional power comes in many different forms: money, authority, gender, and race, to name a few. Here I cannot offer a deep dive into the concept of power, but I can offer a perspective and practice I have come to after many years of building relationships across lines of power.

I believe that a huge inhibitor to living a quality life and achieving transformative community change is the underlying assumption that power is

finite and that in any one community or network of relationships, some people will win, and some will lose.

Yes, positional power is finite. And, yes, civil society needs positional power to function efficiently and effectively. But personal power is infinite and can be recognized and shared consistently within community systems. A culture that fosters the sharing of personal power offers the collective ground needed to support friends and community members in sharing their best gifts and achieving their highest potential. The practice of sharing personal power ensures that positional power is merely a practical instrument and not the dominant frame.

I understand that asking community residents from diverse backgrounds to **share power** seems like a big and perhaps overly optimistic goal. So, instead, think of sharing power as a call for you and others to start a new journey while carrying two items with you along this journey.

The first item you must carry and use on this journey is a **backpack** containing your **unique kernel of power**.

All of us are born with unique qualities to contribute. Any time you meet with a friend, a fellow community member, or hold a small team meeting, make sure you have your **backpack** with you. Even if you do not fully know or understand your **unique kernel of power**, remember that you have it to give, and it is available to you.

The second item to always carry and use is an **empty treasure chest**.

The purpose of this chest is to remind you that you are on a treasure hunt for kernels of power held by your fellow community members. Again, when you sit with someone for a cup of coffee or have a meeting to discuss a particular community issue or initiative, bring your treasure chest and actively seek out the treasures offered to you through your engagement with others.

Over time, if you repeatedly focus on harnessing your personal power while also exploring the personal power of others, you will begin to uncover new resources and solutions that you couldn't have imagined. If you practice sharing power repeatedly, then over time, in interactions with others, you will begin to see the unfolding of a new and transformed community ecosystem.

If you are still feeling skeptical or uncomfortable with the practice of **power sharing**, think of it in terms of four simple behavioral shifts.

SHIFT ONE:
UNDERSTAND YOUR UNIQUE POWER.

What does the old behavior look like?
You enter each new encounter feeling anxious and the need to protect yourself.

What does the new behavior look like?
You enter each new encounter feeling positive, open, and calm.

Why is the shift hard to make?
We have a well-developed story that says we don't have anything to contribute or that others do not appreciate what we have to offer.

SHIFT TWO:
CONTRIBUTE FROM YOUR OWN UNIQUE PERSONAL POWER.

What does this old behavior look like?
You hold back from offering an idea or consume yourself with focusing on and talking about concerns or limiting circumstances.

What does this new behavior look like?
You listen more carefully to creative thoughts that bubble up in your head, and then you take the risk of sharing these thoughts with others.

Why is this shift hard to make?
We have a second well-developed story in our head that tells us things will not go well if we step out and take a risk to share our thoughts.

SHIFT THREE:
BE CURIOUS ABOUT ANOTHER PERSON'S UNIQUE PERSONAL POWER.

What does this old behavior look like?
You consume too much time talking or passively participating, inhibiting others from talking or offering an idea or thought.

What does this new behavior look like?
You talk less and look for opportunities to ask others about their ideas and thoughts.

Why is this shift hard to make?
We often work hard to get our ideas out in the open and don't devote enough energy to drawing out others, especially those who are shy or reticent.

SHIFT FOUR:
RECEIVE OFFERS FROM ANOTHER PERSON'S
UNIQUE PERSONAL POWER.

What does this old behavior look like?
You might immediately disagree, link the offer back to your point, or dismiss it because it does not match what you were looking for.

What does this new behavior look like?
You ask clarifying questions indicating that you heard what someone said and are genuinely interested in knowing more, even if you disagree.

Why is this shift hard to make?
We often hear what people say through our immediate lens, which is usually protective. So, our first instinct is to judge an offer based on how it serves or does not serve our positional interests.

ACTIVE HEART

SHARE POWER

Action and Reflection Prompt

♥ What are two places or situations in your current life where you can try out these shifts?

An Invitation from Me to You

I imagine you have ideas, lessons, and practices not mentioned here. I invite you to use this book mainly as a spark to talk about relationships with others in your midst and how to cultivate relationships where you live and work. And I invite you to share your ideas with me and others in this community of relationship builders. (www.startwiththeheartbooks.com; www.trustedspacepartners.com)

I hope that more of us experience the power of building connections with each other across differences, especially across lines of class and race. Each of us is fully equipped to reach out to someone nearby, learn about them, and connect in small, simple ways.

I wish you much joy and delight as you discover new wisdom and fresh support in the journey of building and cultivating relationships.

WORKS CITED

Blakeslee, Sandra. "Cells That Read Minds." *The New York Times*, The New York Times, 10 Jan. 2006, https://www.nytimes.com/2006/01/10/science/cells-that-read-minds.html.

Brach, Tara. "Tara Brach – a Forgiving Heart: Embracing Our Inner Life (Part 1A)." *YouTube*, YouTube, 15 Jan. 2013, https://www.youtube.com/watch?v=Jx0teElqVYQ.

Braudy, Susan. "He's Woody Allen's 1-1-Silent Partner." *The New York Times*, The New York Times, 21 Aug. 1977, https://www.nytimes.com/1977/08/21/archives/hes-woody-allens-notsosilent-partner.html.

Brown, Brene. *Atlas of the Heart: Mapping Meaningful Connection and the Language of Human Experience,* Random House, 2021.

Cook, Gareth. "Why We Are Wired to Connect." *Scientific American*, Scientific American, 22 Oct. 2013, https://www.scientificamerican.com/article/why-we-are-wired-to-connect/.

Fredrickson, Barbara L. *Love 2.0: How Our Supreme Emotion Affects Everything We Feel, Think, Do, and Become.* Hudson Street Press, 2013.

hooks, bell *all about love: New Visions* William Morrow, 2001.

Jamison, Kaleel. *The Nibble Theory and the Kernel of Power: A Book about Leadership, Self-Empowerment, and Personal Growth.* Paulist Press, 2004.

Kaeufer, Katrin, and Otto Scharmer. *Leading from the Emerging Future: From Ego-System to Eco-System Economies.* Berrett-Koehler, 2013.

Pink, Daniel H. *The Power of Regret: How Looking Backward Moves Us Forward.* Canongate Book Ltd, 2022.

Ross, Howard J. *Everyday Bias: Identifying and Navigating Unconscious Judgments in Our Daily Lives.* Rowman and Littlefield Publishers, 2020.

Ruiz, Miguel, et al. *The Four Agreements: A Practical Guide to Personal Freedom (A Toltec Wisdom Book).* Amber-Allen Pub., 2008.

"The King Philosophy - Nonviolence 365®." The King Center, 25 Feb. 2022, https://thekingcenter.org/about-tkc/the-king-philosophy/.

"The Serenity Prayer and Me." *The Serenity Prayer and Me | Alcoholics Anonymous – Great Britain*, https://www.alcoholics-anonymous.org.uk/Members/Fellowship-Magazines/SHARE-Magazine/December-2019/The-Serenity-Prayer-and-Me.

Thrive. "Who We Are." *Thrive Network*, https://www.thrivenetwork.org/about.

"Use Situation-Behavior-Impact (SBI)™ to Understand Intent." *CCL*, 6 Sept. 2022, https://www.ccl.org/articles/leading-effectively-article/closing-the-gap-between-intent-vs-impact-sbii/.

Here are a list of books, articles, videos, and organizations that have been most helpful to me in my journey of build awareness of and understand the presence, roles, and impacts of white privilege, systemic racism, capitalism, and imperialism.

BOOKS

Jackson Rising: The Struggle for Economic Democracy and Black Self-Determination in Jackson, Mississippi
Kali Akuno and Ajamu Nangwaya, Cooperation Jackson

The New Jim Crow: Mass Incarceration in the Era of Colorblindness
Michelle Alexander

What Then Must We Do? Straight Talk About the Next American Revolution
Gar Alperovitz

Principles of a Pluralist Commonwealth
Gar Alperovitz

Atlas of the Heart: Mapping Meaningful Connection and the Language of Human Experience
Brown, Brene

Between the World and Me
Ta-Nehisi Coates

Love 2.0: How Our Supreme Emotion Affects Everything We Feel, Think, Do, and Become
Barbara L. Frederickson

all about love: New Visions
bell hooks

The Nibble Theory and the Kernel of Power: A Book about Leadership, Self-empowerment, and Personal Growth
Kaleel Jamison

Leading from the Emerging Future: From Ego-System to Eco-System Economies
Katrin Kaufer and Otto Scharmer

Owning Our Future: The Emerging Ownership Revolution
Marjorie Kelly

How To Be an Antiracist
Ibram X. Kendi

This Changes Everything: Capitalism vs. The Climate
Naomi Klein

My Grandmother's Hands: Racialized Trauma and the Pathway to Mending Our Hearts and Bodies
Resmaa Menakem, MSW, LICSW

The Sum of Us: What Racism Costs Everyone and How We Can Prosper Together
Heather McGee

Together. The Healing Power of Human Connection in a Sometimes Lonely World
Vivek H. Murphy, MD

Everyday Bias: Identifying and Navigating Unconscious Judgments in Our Daily Lives
Howard Ross

The Four Agreements: A Practical Guide to Personal Freedom (A Toltec Wisdom Book)
Don Miguel Ruiz

Just Mercy: A Story of Justice and Redemption
Bryan Stevenson

Witnessing Whiteness: The Need to Talk About Whiteness and How to Do It
Shelly Tolchuk

The Warmth of Other Suns
Isabel Wilkerson

Democracy at Work: A Cure for Capitalism
Richard Wolff

PAPERS AND VIDEOS

Everyday Vigilance Required to Make Real Progress Toward Racial Equity & Inclusion
Mark Joseph
youtu.be/n2lingDQoYg

RACE: The Power of an Illusion
California Newsreel
www.racepowerofanillusion.org

White Privilege, "Unpacking the Invisible Backpack"
Peggy McIntosh
https://nationalseedproject.org/about-us/about-seed

White Supremacy Culture
Tema Okun
https://www.whitesupremacyculture.info/

ONLINE COURSES, SITES, COMMUNITIES, AND OTHER RESOURCES

Boston Ujima Project
ujimaboston.com/economybuilders

Center for Economic Democracy
Aaron Tanaka
economicdemocracy.us

The Democracy Collaborative
Gar Alperovitz, Ted Howard, Majorie Kelly
democracycollaborative.org/about

Flourish Agenda and Healing Centered Engagement
Sean Ginwright and Team
flourishagenda.com

Healing from Internalized Whiteness
Wild Seed Society/Sandra Kim
wildseedsociety.com/healing-from-internalized-whiteness

The Kaleel Jamison Consulting Group, Inc.
www.kjcg

Othering and Belonging Institute
john a. powell
belonging.berkeley.edu

Thrive Network
Oakland, California
thrivenetwork.org

White Awake – An Online Resource
https://whiteawake.org/about/
whiteawake.org/themes-and-resources/political-education-resources-for-study-training
You will find many different resources on the **Trusted Space Partners** website.

CALL TO ACTION FOR PLACE-BASED COMMUNITY CHANGE:

My call to action is for teams of neighbors to be creative in forming intentional learning communities across race and class in connection with a specific moment of opportunity and/or shared affinity.

To understand my core conclusion around what is needed for transformative change in neighborhoods, communities, and this world, please read my call to action below for forming intentional learning communities across race and class.

Whether we live in a highly diverse neighborhood in terms of race, class, or culture, or live in a place where most people look like us and have similar educational, cultural, and income profiles, we always face many differences (personality, experiences, gender, sexual orientation, etc.) that must be bridged to build a network of productive relationships. The learning process for effective building and nurturing of different relationships is a lifelong journey.

Many in our society opt out of this developmental process, choosing to go alone or be connected to only a few similar people I do not seek to persuade or influence these people, respecting their personal choices.

Sadly, our country is built on an intentional construct of white supremacy that purposely divides people based on race and class to benefit those with assigned or inherited privilege and to create divisive chaos to ensure this hierarchy of power and privilege continues.

I will not experience the final undoing of this tragic evolution in my lifetime. But I am privileged to have witnessed significant progress towards creating communities where people of highly different backgrounds are in close relationship with each other and are benefiting from reciprocal exchanges of value, working together to change the underlying systems of inequity.

As I observe and participate in these moments of progress, I notice the repeated presence of certain beliefs, attitudes, knowledge, and skills that support building trust, collaborative action, and change. This list is ever evolving and not linear but includes the following elements:

- Belief in/Love of Self
- An Aspirational Mindset and Clarity of Purpose
- Core Communication Skills

- Knowledge of Racial/Class/Cultural History and Current Conditions
- Personal Awareness of Impact of Racial, Class, and Cultural Privileges
- Personal Awareness of Impact of Racial, Class, and Cultural Trauma

- Access to Intentional and Safe Spaces for Connection
- Intentional Practices of Connection, Mutual Exchange, and Relationship Building

- Belief in Interdependence as the Natural Order
- Intentional Practices and Spaces for Interdependence and Shared Action

I have further observed—through action learning—that the most effective, and perhaps only, way to pursue this developmental path is in an intentional learning community with others who bring a wide array of backgrounds and life experiences. I urge those of you who are the convenors of community to explore how to create and support ongoing intentional learning communities, wherever you are and in whatever moment of opportunity presents itself.

ABOUT THE AUTHOR

For over 40 years, Frankie has explored how reliable and trusted relationships can provide a helpful web of both support and accountability, for individuals and for communities, in an increasingly fast paced and unpredictable world. In 2011, Frankie co-founded Trusted Space Partners, working with activists and organizations across the country. Prior to this, she was the founder and executive director of Impact Silver Spring, sparking a new network of over 1,000 people of all different racial, cultural, and socio-economic backgrounds working for social change in Silver Spring, Maryland. Frankie's interest in how to cultivate networks of impactful relationships has been a common thread through a career of over 30 years in public interest law, affordable housing, community development and public and nonprofit management. She currently lives in Saxapahaw, North Carolina.